A PICTURE OF

STOCKPORT

IN CHESHIRE

A COLLECTION OF PHOTOGRAPHS

by

H.LEES

Introduction by

WILLIAM J. SKILLERN, F.L.A.

1971
Published by
E. J. MORTEN, Didsbury, Manchester 20.

First Published December 1970 by
E. J. Morten (Publishers), Warburton Street,
Didsbury, Manchester 20.

O ISBN 901598 19 4

Printed by The Acorn Press, 10 Pall Mall, Liverpool L3 6HJ.

Author

Title

INTRODUCTION

Like any other town of 140,000 inhabitants spread over 8,400 acres, Stockport shows a variety of faces in a variety of places. To many outsiders it is just another northern mill town. Many of its old mills are still standing, though now given over to industries other than cotton spinning, and the modern science of industrial archaeology is increasingly anxious to record their structures by photographs and measurements.

But Stockport existed long before the Industrial Revolution and in 1970 celebrated the 750th anniversary of the granting of its first Charter in 1220. The oldest part of its present Parish Church was in existence in 1334; its Market dates from 1260, its Grammar School from 1487. Two sixteenth-century houses stand in Great Underbank – one a bank, the other a restaurant. In Middle Hillgate is a house with downspout dated 1715 – the year of the Old Pretender's rising; thirty years later his son, Bonny Prince Charlie, passed through Stockport.

All these events took place long before the invention of photography, and the present selection, almost all from the camera of Harry Lees, shows the Stockport scene of modern times. Mr. Lees, who is grateful to those friends who have allowed their photographs to be copied, is a Stockport man who is very conversant with his native town and for over forty years has devoted much of his spare time to photographing it and processing his own films. He is Historical Records Secretary of Stockport Photographic Society and was one of the earliest members of Stockport Historical Society. He has an eye for the unusual, the quaint and the historic, and the present work is a small selection from the hundreds of photographs he has taken. If it be thought that some of his street scenes lack the bustle of everyday Stockport life, this is because he finds it convenient to confine most of his photography to Sunday mornings.

Many street scenes and facets of the town's life are presented in these pictures, together with some scenes from the not so distant past. Do you remember the river before the bold plan of building Merseyway over it was carried out? Do you recall the electric trams which ran for just fifty years until their demise in 1951? Or the cinemas and railway stations that have disappeared within the last dozen years? Some of these are pictured on the following pages and will stir the memories of Stockportonians everywhere.

The situation of Stockport, with its town centre in the gorge formed by the River Mersey, gives it a more varied topography than most other towns. Steep streets climb out of the river valley and in two places a bridge is necessary to carry one road over another. The main road through the town, the A6, is a good wide road but some side streets are still paved with setts. Stockport's pride is undoubtedly its splendid new shopping precinct at Merseyway, with its modern two-level shops linked by stairs, lifts and escalators. The original designers of Merseyway as a major road for through traffic could hardly have imagined that thirty years later it would be used by pedestrians only.

Stockport.
November, 1970.

WILLIAM J. SKILLERN.

VERNON BRIDGE

Before Merseyway was completed in 1940, this pedestrian way over the river connected the two sections of Union Road. Photographed about 1937.

Above: Looking towards Underbank.

Below: Looking towards Prince's Street, with the Palladium Cinema in the Background.

ODD CORNERS IN STOCKPORT

Top right: A decorated lead downspout, Middle Hillgate.

Below: Old Road, or Dodge Hill, at its junction with Lancashire Hill.

Bottom right: Pearson's Court, behind High Bank Side, in the late 1950's.

Below: Metal post, bearing the Borough Arms, erected to prevent vehicles using Pickford's Brow, leading off St. Peter's Square.

ASTOR CINEMA (FORMERLY HIPPODROME)

Left: The side entrance in High Street, with traces of poster announcing its last film, "A Bucket of Blood", before it was burnt out in 1960.

Below: The awning marks the rather insignificant entrance in St. Petersgate.

Below: From Adlington Square, showing how the Astor stood above adjoining houses, as well as the shops in Underbank.

RAILWAY VIADUCT

Stockport's town centre is dominated by the massive viaduct, 1786 feet long and 111 feet high. As recorded on the tablet below, it was built in 21 months and completed on December 21st, 1840, but remained unused until the Manchester & Birmingham Railway was extended from Heaton Norris to Sandbach on May 10th, 1842. It was widened to four tracks in 1887-9.

Above: Stockholm Road, crossing the Crewe railway line at "Monkey Bridge". In the background are the spire of St. Matthew's Church, Edgeley, and the floodlighting towers of Stockport County Football Ground.

Below: These old tiled cottages stood on the A6 road opposite Bramhall Lane until demolished in the 1960's.

Above: One of Stockport's cinemas was The King's, which stood in Bentley Street, off Lancashire Hill.

Top right: A view down Lord Street, with St. Peter's Church at the bottom.

Above: Prince's Street and a corner of Mersey Square.

Left: Wellington Road South, below the Infirmary, in 1960.

Above: Varying roof levels and building styles in Chestergate.

Left and below: Two views of Great Underbank showing the 16th century town house of the Leghs of Adlington, now a restaurant.

STATIONS NO MORE

Above: Tiviot Dale, opened in 1865, was a passenger station for 101 years.

Left: The suburban station at Heaton Mersey was in business from 1880 to 1961.

Right: Heaton Norris, closed here in 1959, is here shown during demolition.

Below: The pleasing exterior of Tiviot Dale, demolished in 1968. Behind is Hanover Congregational Chapel.

FIRE ! FIRE !

These reproductions of old photographs show horse-drawn and motorised fire appliances and a horse-drawn police ambulance, all outside the old Fire Station in Mersey Square. In December 1926, the "Mary Dalziel" (below) went over Wellington Bridge, killing Superintendent Beckwith (seated, on right).

Above: Post-war pre-fab bungalows at Whitehill, which were demolished to provide a site for the new 1967 Fire Station (left and below).

Bottom: The 1962 offices of the Stockport & District Water Board, with the Tower of St. Peter's Church in the background.

Left: A Stockport tramcar in Newbridge Lane in 1927.

Below: North Western buses parked on spare ground between A6 and the Viaduct.

Left: An unusual visitor about 1956 was this Westland S55 Whirlwind helicopter, which landed on Heaton Norris Recreation Ground.

Advertising on two, three or four wheels. These hand-carts and delivery vehicles had bodies made by a local firm. The horse-drawn milk float was photographed in Bradstone Road in 1961.

Solid-tyres vehicles of the past. A breakdown lorry in Heaton Lane Transport Depot in the late 1950's, and the transport fleet of Robinson's Brewery in the early 'twenties. Note the three steam lorries at the far end.

ABOVE THE ROOF-TOPS

Top: Looking East from the Fire Station, about 1930.

Centre: From the same view point in 1967, looking North-East.

Bottom: Looking South from Heaton Norris Recreation Ground, after demolition of property in Bridgefield Street.

Above and below: The entrances to two Courts off Penny Lane, the lower one also giving access to the backs of houses on Lancashire Hill.

SOME STOCKPORT STEPS

Above: Crowther Street, off Lower Hillgate, has been painted by several artists, including L. S. Lowry. The houses were taken down in 1960.

Below: These steps off Lancashire Hill bear the name Roman Road.

MORE STEPS

Left: Lavender Brow in 1959, looking up to Churchgate.

Right: Bank Steps, with gas lamp, leading up from Little Underbank.

Bottom left: These steps in Port Street gave access to Stewart Street beyond the archway.

Bottom right: Not far away, Heaton Norris Recreation Ground could be reached by these steps.

Above: Hanover Congregational Chapel, built 1821, closed 1962, demolished 1966.

Left: The War Memorial Art Gallery, 1925.

Right: The Infirmary, 1833, with the extension of 1938.

Work on the Merseyway complex was spread over many years. The top photograph shows the temporary pathway which connected the two sections of Union Street in 1965 during the building of the shopping precinct. Below are two views of the alterations in Mersey Square in the early thirties, which resulted in the construction of the "Bear Pit". This was the real beginning of the Merseyway complex.

The major contruction work of the middle thirties was the complete bridging of the river between Mersey Square and Lancashire Bridge. The result was Merseyway, opened in September, 1940.

Right: Lamb's Fold Cottages, Heaton Norris, with headstone dated 1793.

Left: Manchester Road in 1961, showing Bethesda Methodist Chapel (closed in 1967).

Right: Another view in Manchester Road. A few of these houses formerly had cellar dwellings.

Left: Pre-fabs on Whitehill estate in 1959. The new Fire Station now stands on this site.

Above: This row of terraced houses in Brunswick Street, off Georges Road, included a public house with the same name.

Right: One of Stockport's "Brows" or steep narrow streets leading to the Market Place, in 1960. The Albion Hotel at the bottom was formerly the Sun and is now converted into a jeweller's shop.

Business premises of the past. Barber's were in Wellington Road North, Arnfield's backed on to Merseyway, the blacksmith was in Bridgefield Street and the "Lurry" works was in Wellington Road North before the first world war.

Above: The Exchange Street corner of Wellington Road South, opposite St. Petersgate, in 1960, before modernisation and widening.

Above: Immediately above Exchange Street was the Super Cinema, built 1910 and demolished in 1968.

Left: Hoardings and business premises on the North side of Prince's Street about 1912.

Top: The full length of the railway viaduct is seen above the chimney pots in this view from Bowerfold Lane, Heaton Norris, in 1961.

Centre: The town centre and Heaton Norris Rec., as seen from a viewpoint near Stockport Station.

Bottom: Looking North towards Reddish from the flats at Lincoln Towers, Hillgate, in 1967, after demolition on Lancashire Hill and Penny Lane.

The Market Place – always a busy spot on Fridays and Saturdays. In the top picture, the soldiers' uniforms and women's dresses indicate a war-time scene; 1942, in fact. The lower picture shows a wet day in the post-war period.

St. Peter's Square, with the Theatre Royal on the right.

Demolition of Theatre Royal in 1962.

Mersey Square in the early 1930's, when some buses carried destination boards above the windows.

The Plaza Cinema in Mersey Square (now a Bingo Hall).

Higher Hillgate, with the lodge of the former Christy's Hatworks (now associated British Hat Manufacturers) on the right.

Left: Looking North from St. Petersgate bridge into Union Street before the shopping precinct was started.

Right: Lower Hillgate, which was part of the principal road through the town until 1826.

Left: A supermarket and building society offices now stand on the site of the old Theatre Royal in St. Peter's Square.

OLD AND NEW

Above: Round doorways and obtrusive advertisements on Wellington Road North, just above Mersey Square, in 1961.

Below and right: Square-cornered high-rise and low-rise flats on Lancashire Hill.

MODERN CORPORATION HOUSING ESTATES

Lancashire Hill flats.

These flats overlooking the Recreation Ground carry the appropriate names of Heaton Towers and Norris Towers.

Shopping centre at Brinnington.

Left: Delaney's Buildings, a row of 19th century cottages below road level in Wellington Street, were taken down in the early 1960's.

Below: Another view of Lancashire Hill flats on the left, and two pictures of houses and flats at Brinnington.

MERSEYWAY SHOPPING PRECINCT

The Western end of the precinct, with escalators and balconies.

The new Mersey Square entrance to Merseyway.

Another view, showing the curved arcading where the round arches of the Fire Station once stood.

Pendlebury Hall, Tiviot Dale Station and the mills of Portwood beyond.

Stockport by night, from Bowerfold Lane, Heaton Norris.

Looking Southwards from Heaton Norris. On the skyline, the Sunday School, Mottram Street flats and the Town Hall.

Another view from Heaton Norris, showing St. Mary's Church and the shopping centre.

Shopping precinct under construction on both sides of Merseyway in 1967.

A bird's-eye view of Middle Hillgate, showing its intersection with Edward Street and Waterloo Road.

View towards New Zealand Road and Vernon Park, from above Peak Street.

This was the view Southwards from Heaton Norris in 1961.

Mills and foliage in Hope's Carr, just East of Middle Hillgate.

Left: The exterior of the Town Hall underwent a thorough cleaning in the Summer of 1968.

Right: A closer view of the scaffolding and sheeting used during the cleaning.

Left: The job completed.

Left: The Underbank entrance to the Merseyway car park.

Right: Entrance to car park and view over Underbank.

Left: Top level of car park, with clock tower and Co-operative Society building.

MERSEYWAY SHOPPING PRECINCT

Left: Escalators at the Western end of the precinct (must be a Sunday!)

Right: Adlington Walk, the principal entrance from Chestergate / Underbank.

Left: The escalators in use and shoppers everywhere.

More local delivery vehicles. Sutton & Co. were well known as carriers between Stockport and Manchester. The milk cart belonged to Nixon's of Woodhall Farm, Reddish, and was photographed on Sandy Lane in 1959.

MODERN BUILDINGS

Top left: Shopping centre at Brinnington.

Top right: Holborn House (Inland Revenue) in John Street, with the Centenary Hall of Stockport Sunday School in the background.

Bottom: The "Jack and Jill" public house at Brinnington.

Top: Another night-time view from Bowerfold Lane.

Centre: Tiviot Dale Station, the electricity works and Portwood Mills.

Bottom: Looking North from High Bank Side over Merseyway towards Heaton Norris in 1960.

A high-level view of Mersey Square.

The approach to Mersey Square from Wellington Road North.

Lancashire Hill in 1962, before demolition of property.

Above: Hope's Carr, looking towards Wellington Street, with part of two old mills on the right.

Curate Street, off Turncroft Lane, had this early stone street sign dated 1807. It is now in Stockport Museum.

Right: A glimpse of the Mersey at Lancashire Bridge, with Park Mills opposite.

STONEWORK IN STOCKPORT

Left: Old drinking fountain in Vernon Park.

Below: A piece of modern sculpture at the Underbank entrance of Adlington Walk.

Stone plaque on Tiviot Dale Station, bearing the initials of the Manchester, Sheffield & Lincolnshire, Great Northern, and Midland Railways. It is now in Stockport Museum.

Left: The tower of St. Mary's Parish Church in the Market Place, floodlit in the 1930's.

Right: This bandstand stood in Vernon Park until it was removed in the 1960's.

PLAN OF STOCKPORT, 1824

The plan which appears overleaf is reproduced from the separate volume of "Illustrations" to Edward Baines' "History, directory and gazetteer of the County Palatine of Lancaster", published at Liverpool in two volumes in 1824-25.

At that time the town was entirely on the Cheshire side of the Mersey and the text on Stockport was printed as an Appendix at the end of Volume 2. Baines began rather apologetically by saying *"Though not strictly within the prescribed limits of this work, Stockport is so closely connected both by trade and local situation with the county of Lancaster as to claim a brief notice"*, then went on to devote 14 pages to it.

The town was surveyed by R. Thornton in 1824 and the result is important because it is the first accurately detailed street plan of Stockport to be published – or at least is the earliest one known. The course of the Mersey is correctly shown, but Portwood Reservoir and Carr Dam have long since disappeared. Both the "New Road" (Wellington Road) and St. Thomas' Church were still under construction when the plan was drawn. A number of the streets illustrated in this present volume are shown, and virtually all the streets leading off Hillgate bear the same names today as they did nearly 150 years ago.

Surveyed by R. Thornton.

Surveyed 1824, for Baines La